W9-CDN-629

KAYAKING, CANOEING, ROWING, AND YACHTING

A TRUE BOOK

by

Christian Ditchfield

Children's Press®
A Division of Grolier Publishing

New York London Hong Kong Sydney
Danbury, Connecticut

Sailboarding

Reading Consultant
Linda Cornwell
*Coordinator of School Quality
and Professional Improvement
Indiana State Teachers
Association*

*The photo on the cover shows
a kayaker during a whitewater
rodeo. The photo on the title
page shows a woman kayaker.*

Note to the reader:
*In canoeing, kayaking, and rowing
competitions, the metric system is
used to measure distances. Here's
a metric-conversion website you
can visit to help you convert
kilometers to miles:*
http://tqjunior.advanced.org/3804

Visit Children's Press® on
the Internet at:
http://publishing.grolier.com

Library of Congress Cataloging-in-Publication Data

Ditchfield, Christin.
   Kayaking, canoeing, rowing, and yachting / by Christin Ditchfield.
       p.   cm. — (A true book)
   Includes bibliographical references (p.   ) and index.
   Summary: Describes the equipment and techniques of kayaking,
canoeing, rowing, and yachting.
   ISBN 0-516-21610-4 (lib. bdg.)   0-516-27024-9 (pbk.)
   1. Boats and boating Juvenile literature. [1. Boats and boating.]
I. Title. II. Series.
GV775.3.D58   2000
797.1—dc21   99-28207
                                                                    CIP
                                                                     AC

GROLIER
PUBLISHING

Contents

A racing sailboat

On the Water

People have been boating for thousands of years. In the beginning, it was strictly for transportation. Canoes, kayaks, and sailboats were used to carry people and goods from one place to another. Hunters, explorers, and traders traveled by boat to places they couldn't

Eleventh-century drawing of a Greek fishing boat

reach on foot. Fishermen
went out to sea in search of
a good catch.

Nowadays, people go boating for fun and relaxation. And of course, boating is a very popular sport. Athletes who

In some kinds of boat racing, the athletes must battle rough waters.

compete in water sports need to be good swimmers. They must also be very strong in order to steer, paddle, or row their boats. There are many safety rules to learn.

Competitions can be intense—and even dangerous. Boaters battle the wind and the waves, as well as their opponents. But the thrill of victory makes it all seem worthwhile.

Canoeing

Long ago, North American
Indians invented canoeing.
They made boats from bark,
animal skins, and hollowed-
out tree trunks. Canoes today
are made of aluminum and
fiberglass, but the design is
the same as those early
Indian canoes.

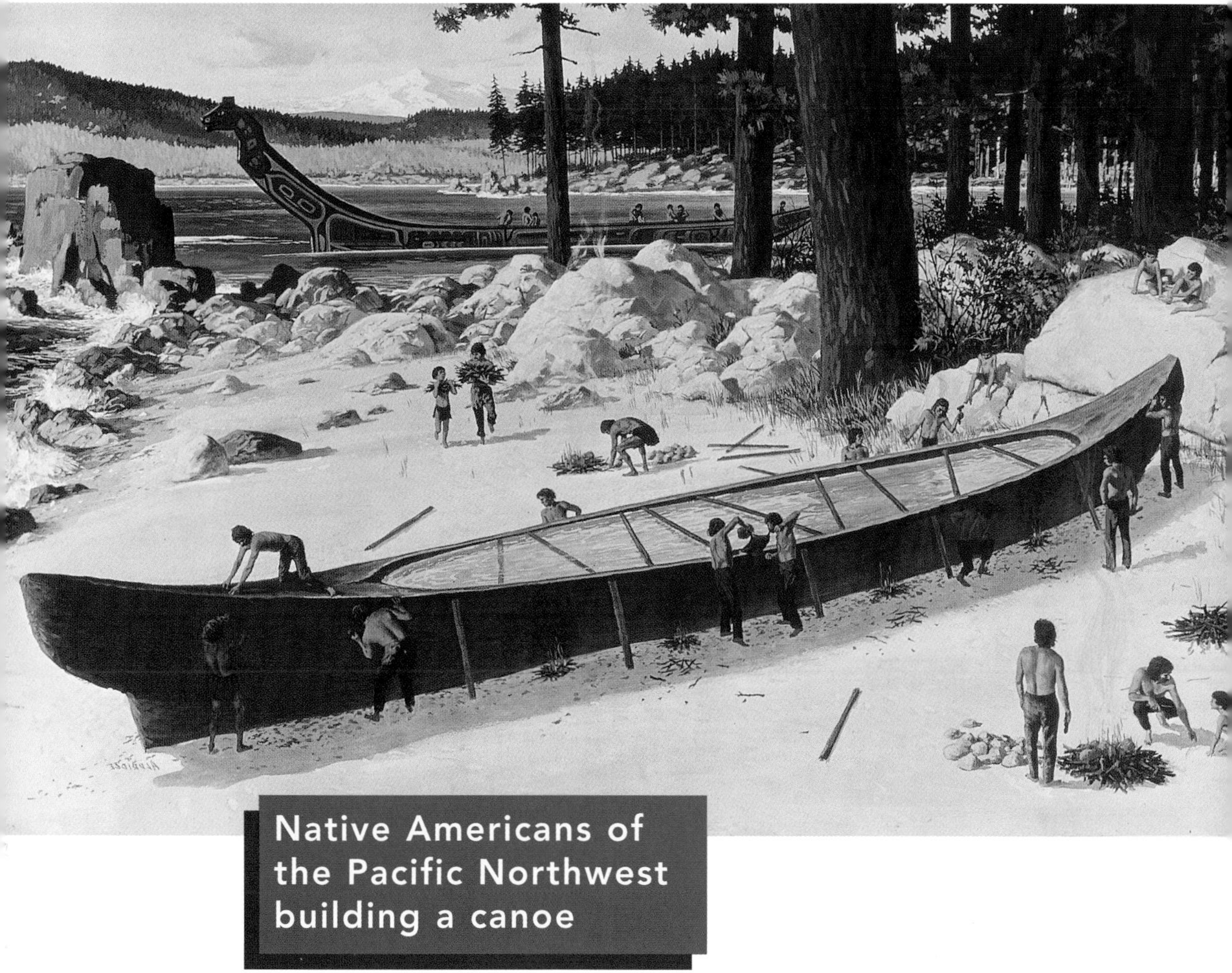

Native Americans of
the Pacific Northwest
building a canoe

Canoeists kneel in the bottom of the boat and use a one-bladed paddle.

A canoe is a small open boat that is pointed at both ends. These boats have no sails or motors. They are sturdy but lightweight. The boater kneels in the bottom of the canoe and propels the boat through the water by using a paddle with a blade on one end.

Competitive canoeing involves many different races and events. Two types of events are included in the Summer Olympic Games: sprints and whitewater slaloms. Only men compete in canoeing in the Olympics.

Sprints take place on "flat water"—water without waves—

A men's doubles team competing in an Olympic sprint canoe race

and are done in a straight line, with competitors assigned to lanes. These races cover distances of 500 to 1,000 meters.

Whitewater races are held in fast, rough waters over courses at least 3 kilometers long. The rocky terrain above and below the water makes it hard for the competitors to maneuver.

The slalom is by far the most difficult and dangerous white-water event. For this reason, all slalom competitors wear life jackets and protective helmets.

A slalom course is 600 meters long. The canoeist has to pass through twenty-five

An Olympic whitewater
slalom course

slalom gates while avoiding
rocks and currents. The
"gates" are multicolored
poles suspended from wires
in the air. A competitor who

misses a gate receives penalty points. The winner is the athlete with the fastest time and the fewest penalty points.

Canoeists maneuvering through a slalom gate

Kayaking

Kayaks were first used by Inuit hunters in Canada, Alaska, and northern Russia. These boats are much like canoes— small, narrow, and lightweight. A kayak, however, has a closed deck. The kayaker sits in a small opening called a cockpit.

This is a traditional Inuit kayak (top). Kayakers sit rather than kneel in their boats (above). Some kayaks hold up to four people (left).

Some kayaks hold up to four people. These boats have a separate cockpit for each

Kayakers use a paddle with a blade on each end.

person. Kayakers use paddles with two blades, one on each end of the stick.

Modern kayakers wear wet suits to help them stay warm and dry. A rubber skirt called a spraydeck keeps water out of the boat.

One of the most important skills a kayaker learns is the "roll." Small boats often flip over in rough water, but a good kayaker can use a paddle to roll over and turn right-side up—without getting out of the boat.

A kayaker doing a "roll"

A kayak slalom race

Kayaking competitions are part of the Summer Olympics. Kayakers compete in sprints, whitewater races, and slaloms. Both men's and women's kayaking events are included in the Olympics.

Wild Water Sport

Kayakers all over the world are competing in a wacky new sport called whitewater rodeo. These daring athletes twirl their paddles in the air while performing acrobatic stunts like the "loop," the "pirouette," and the "cartwheel grab." Judges award points for style, skill, and creativity.

Kayaker doing a "pirouette" during a whitewater rodeo

Rowing

Long before sails were invented, boats were propelled through the water by rowing. Thousands of years ago, ancient Egyptians forced slaves to row their giant barges down the Nile River. The ancient Greeks and Romans put prisoners of

Ancient Greek stone carving showing men rowing a warship (above); a World Championship of Rowing competition (left)

war to work in the same way.
Now, people row boats
purely for fun and sport.

The lightweight boats used in rowing sports are called "shells." Shells can be anywhere from 24 feet (7.3 m) to 60 feet (18.3 m) long. They are usually made of such materials as Kevlar, graphite, or ultrathin plywood.

Each crew member uses two hands to row one oar—a "sweep oar." In a type of racing called scull racing, each crew member handles two oars called "sculling oars." This type of rowing is also known as "sculling."

A women's quadruple-scull race

Martha S. Ferguson

It takes great strength and skill to maneuver oars quickly and smoothly through the water. A crew must work as a team to time their strokes together. Without rhythm, their movements will be awkward and useless.

A crew must work as a team to time their strokes perfectly.

The Head of the Charles Regatta is a famous rowing competition.

In a rowing competition, the races are divided into categories according to the number of crew members in the boat. Sculling races may feature one, two, or four rowers. Shell races require teams of two, four, or eight rowers.

Unlike canoers and kayak- ers, rowers don't face the direction in which they are going, but rather look like they are rowing "backwards."

Sometimes there is an extra team member in the boat called a coxswain (pronounced "coxs'n"). The coxswain does not row. Instead, he or she sits facing forward in the back of the shell to steer. The coxswain also calls out directions to

A coxswain sits in the back of the shell and faces forward.

the crew and helps them keep their rhythm going as they row.

Men's coxed eights competing in the World Rowing Championships

Races with coxswains are said to be "coxed"—as in "coxed pairs" or "coxed fours." Races that do not include a coxswain are called "coxless." In coxless races, one of the crew members steers the shell with a pedal at his feet.

The most prestigious rowing competitions take place at the World Championships and the Olympic Games. In the Olympic Games, men and women compete in fourteen rowing events. Each race is held on a lake and covers a distance of 2,000 meters.

Yachting

Yachts are sailboats that are fast and easy to handle. These boats move quickly through the water, powered by the wind pushing against their sails. A yacht may be sailed by one person—or by twenty.

Yachts come in all shapes and sizes. They include sailboards,

A racing sailboat keeling to the side in rough seas

Sailboards (top),
a dinghy in a race
(above), and a
catamaran (right)

dinghies, and catamarans. The boats are built from plastic, aluminum, and carbon fiber. The sails are made of nylon and other lightweight fabrics.

Yacht races, called regattas, take place in lakes, rivers, and oceans. A regatta may be a point-to-point race or a closed-course race. In a point-to-point race, the boats go from one specific place to another. For example, boaters in the TransPac race sail from

A closed-course race (above) and the Whitbread Round the World Race (left)

California to Hawaii. In a closed-course race, the competitors sail around an island or a buoy or some other type of marker and then head back again.

The most famous yacht race is the America's Cup. This closed-course race began in 1851, and is held every four years. The course is 24 miles (39 km) long. Over the years,

A sailboat competing in the America's Cup

yachts from many nations have competed for the honor of winning this trophy.

Yachting is also an important part of the Olympic Games. The races are divided into eight classes, depending on the type of boat and the number of crew members. The race classes for individual competitors are the Mistral, Laser, Europe, and Finn. Teams of two can compete in the 470 class,

A parade of women's 470 sailors during an Olympic competition

Star class, and Tornado class.
The Soling class is for teams
of three people.

Yachting is one of the few Olympic sports in which men and women can race side by side. Mixed teams may compete in the Tornado, Laser, and 470 classes.

Each class holds seven races during the Olympics. Teams earn points based on how they finish in each race. The first-place team receives zero points, the second-place finisher wins three points, and so on. At the end of all seven races, the points will be added up. The team with the lowest score wins the gold medal.

Gold-medal-winning 470-class sailors during the 1996 Olympics

To Find Out More

Here are some additional resources to help you learn more about kayaking, canoeing, rowing, and yachting:

Books

Bailey, Donna. **Canoeing.** Steck-Vaughn Company, 1991.

Bailey, Donna. **Sailing.** Steck-Vaughn Company, 1991.

Fox, Alan. **Kayaking.** Lerner Publications Company, 1993.

Kalman, Bobbie. **A Canoe Trip.** Crabtree Publishing Company, 1995.

Thomas, Ron and Joe Herran. **The Grolier Student Encyclopedia of the Olympic Games.** Grolier Educational, 1996.

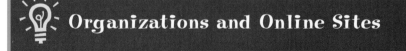

Organizations and Online Sites

International Olympic Committee (IOC)
http://www.olympic.org

This page can tell you about the organization that runs all Olympic Games.

United States Olympic Committee (USOC)
Olympic House
One Olympic Plaza
Colorado Springs, CO
80909-5760
http://www.usoc.org

The United States Olympic Committee supervises Olympic activity for the United States. Its website includes everything you want to know about Olympic sports, past and present.

United States Rowing Association
Pan American Plaza,
Suite 400
201 South Capitol Ave.
Indianapolis, IN 46225
http://www.usrowing.org

The U.S. Rowing Association provides opportunities for all people to experience rowing—from recreation to Olympic victory. Its website provides details on upcoming U.S. rowing events.

USA Team C-1
http://usac-1.8m.com/

This is the official site of the National C-1 Whitewater Rodeo Team. It features pages on each member, as well as photos.

Important Words

buoy floating object used to mark a spot in the water

catamaran boat having twin hulls that are side by side

crew members of a racing team

dinghy small sailboat

fiberglass strong material made of glass spun into very thin threads

keeling leaning

maneuver to move skillfully

sailboard modified surfboard that has a mast mounted on it and is sailed by one person standing up

slalom zigzag or wavy course between upright obstacles

wet suit tight rubber suit that keeps people warm in cold water

white water foaming, rushing water

Index

Meet the Author

Christin Ditchfield is the author of several books for Children's Press, including five True Books on the Summer Olympics. Her interviews with celebrity athletes have appeared in magazines all over the world. Ms. Ditchfield makes her home in Sarasota, Florida.